Eyewitness Accounts of the American Revolution

A Family Narrative
Francis H. Brooke

The New York Times & Arno Press

Reprint Edition 1971 by Arno Press Inc.

*

LC# 74-140856
ISBN 0-405-01196-2

*

Eyewitness Accounts of the American Revolution, Series III
ISBN for complete set: 0-405-01187-3

*

Manufactured in the United States of America

A
FAMILY NARRATIVE

Being the Reminiscences of a Revolutionary Officer

Afterwards Judge of the Court of Appeals

Written for the information of his children

By FRANCIS J. BROOKE

Sometime Captain in Harrison's Regiment of Artillery

RICHMOND, VA.:

MACFARLANE & FERGUSSON

1849

TARRYTOWN, N. Y.

REPRINTED

WILLIAM ABBATT

1921

Being Extra Number 74 of the Magazine of History with Notes and Queries, Pages 1 - 44.

A FAMILY NARRATIVE

OF

A REVOLUTIONARY OFFICER

FRANCIS J. BROOKE

MACFARLANE & FERGUSSON

PRINTERS,

RICHMOND, VIRGINIA.

1849

EDITOR'S PREFACE.

OUR first item is an unusual one—a family memoir, written by a father for his children and issued as a private publication, in a very small edition: so small that its existence is almost unknown, but one copy being recorded as sold, in many years.

The author was a distinguished lawyer and judge of Virginia, who had joined Washington's army at sixteen, and after the Revolution held various judicial offices, including that of judge of the Court of Appeals, which he held for forty years.

His nephew, and one of his brothers were also distniguished as soldiers, while of a second brother we printed an interesting account in our EXTRA No. 21, he having been a surgeon on the *Bon Homme Richard*, with John Paul Jones.

One of the most interesting features of the book is its notice of Washington. Judge Brooke was on intimate terms with him, and shows that he could unbend in society to an extent which reveals him in a light infinitely more human than any heretofore shown by any one else.

Yet he says "the next day, when I went to his sister's (Mrs. Fielding Lewis') to introduce strangers to him, I found him one of the most dignified men of the age—there was a sublimity in his greatness which exceeded that of any of the great men of ancient or modern history."

Our second item has never before been reprinted. It is an excessively rare piece of early New England poetry (an original is priced at $85, in a list before us), and is directed against Governor Francis Bernard ("St. Francisco").

An even greater interest attaches to it, as one of the only three poems known to have been written by Dr. Benjamin Church, "the first American traitor." One of the others we have already re-published (see "The Choice," in our issue No. 68) and both show the author to have been a man of talent and poetic feeling.

It will be noticed that it has no place or printer's name attached: doubtless no such would wish to be prosecuted by the angry Governor; but it was probably printed in Boston in 1769.

TO
MY BELOVED DAUGHTER HELEN
Who has been my amanuensis in preparing this Family
Narrative,—has written about two-thirds of it from
my dictation,—and aided me essentially in com-
pleting it;— I now most affectionately
dedicate it, with my paternal
blessing.
FRANCIS J. BROOKE.

Richmond, May 1st, 1849.

A FAMILY NARRATIVE

I WAS born on the 27th of August, 1763, at Smithfield, the residence of my beloved father, upon the Rappahannock, four miles below Fredericksburg. Tradition said it was called Smithfield after Capt. John Smith, otherwise called Pocahontas Smith; but as there is nothing in the histories of Virginia stating that Capt. Smith was ever so high up the Rappahannock, I think that tradition was in error. I think it was so called after a Capt. Laurence Smith, who in 1679 had a military commission to defend the frontier against the Indians in that region. It was an estate belonging to one Tanner, who was in England, and authorized his agent to sell it, and it was bought by my grandfather, Taliaferro, who then resided at Epsom, the adjoining estate, and he gave it to my mother— God bless her. The estate now belongs to Mr. Thomas Pratt: the old house in which I was born is burnt down, and he has built a new one, not so large, and higher up the river. When I was a boy there were the traces of a fortification, including a fine spring, as a defense against Indians.

My father was the youngest son of my grandfather, who came to this country with a Mr. Beverly, at the time Gov. Spotswood came, about the year 1715; he became the Surveyor of the State, and was with the Governor when he first crossed the Blue Ridge, for which he received from the Executive a medal, a gold horse-shoe set with garnets and worn as a brooch, which I have seen in the possession of Edmund Brooke, who belonged to the oldest branch of the family.

My father's name was Richard Brooke. He left four sons and a daughter by my mother, and a fifth son by his second wife; he died aged sixty of gout in the stomach, in the year 1792. He was a handsome man, as may be seen by his picture which I have; great vivacity of spirits; he read much; had a good library of the books of that age. He sent my two eldest brothers, Laurence and Robert, at an early age, to Edinburgh college, where they were educated for the two learned professions, Medicine and Law, and did not return to this country until the Revolution had progressed. They got over to France, and Dr. Brooke was appointed by Dr. Franklin, Surgeon of the *Bon Homme Richard*, commanded by the celebrated John Paul Jones, and was in the battle with the *Serapis*, and all the battles of that memorable cruise.

My brother Robert was captured and carried into New York, and sent back to England by Lord Howe, went again to Scotland, again got over to France, and returned to Virginia in a French frigate that brought the arms supplied by the French government. He did not remain idle, but joined a volunteer troop of cavalry under Capt. Larkin Smith, was captured in a charge of dragoons by a Capt. Loller, of Symcoe's Queen's Rangers, at Westham, seven miles above Richmond; he was soon exchanged; commenced the practice of law; was a member of the House of Delegates, and in 1794 was elected Governor of the State, and afterwards Attorney General, in opposition to Bushrod Washington, who was afterwards a Judge of the Supreme Court of the U. States. My brother Robert died while Attorney General, in the year 1799. Dr. Brooke died some years after, I do not recollect the year.

My father was devoted to the education of his children. He sent my twin brother John, and myself very young to school. We went to several English schools, some of them at home, and at nine years of age were sent to the Grammar school in Fredericksburg, taught by a Trinity gentleman from Dublin, by the name of Lennegan, who having left the country at the commencement of the war of the Revolution, was hanged for Petit Treason, and being sentenced to be quartered after he was cut down, was only gashed down the thighs and arms and delivered to his mother, afterwards came to life, got over to England, was smuggled over to France, being a Catholic, and died in the monastery of La Trappe: (according to Jonah Barrington, in whose work this account of him will be found.) My father sent us to other Latin and Greek schools, but finally engaged a private tutor—a Scotch gentleman of the name of Alexander Dunham, by whom we were taught Latin and Greek. He was an amiable man, but entirely ignorant of every thing but Latin and Greek, in which he was a ripe scholar. We read with him all the higher classics; I read Juvenal and Persius with great facility, and some Greek—the Testament and Æsop's Fables.

Having passed the age of sixteen, the military age of that period, I was appointed a first Lieutenant in Gen. Harrison's regiment of Artillery, the last of the year 1780; and my twin brother, not liking to part with me, shortly after got the commission of first Lieutenant in the same regiment. Our first campaign was under the Marquis La Fayette, in the year 1781, during the invasion of Lord Cornwallis. We came to Richmond in March of that year, and were ordered to go on board an old sloop with a mulatto Captain. She was loaded with cannon and military stores, destined to repair the fortification at Portsmouth, which had been destroyed the winter before by the traitor General Arnold. She dropped down the river to Curles, where we were put on board, with the stores of the twenty gun ship the *Renown*, commanded by Commodore Lewis, of Fredericksburg; in addition to which ship there were two other square-rigged vessels and an armed schooner. We were detained some days lying before Curles, the residence of Mr. Richard Randolph, who treated us with great hospitality, we being often on shore.

In about ten days the ship was hailed from the opposite bank, by Major North, one of the aids of the Baron Steuben, who was then at Chesterfield Court-House. Major North was brought on board the ship: he informed Commodore Lewis that the British fleet was in Hampton Roads, and ordered him to put the artillery and stores on the north bank of the river, and to run the ship and the rest of the fleet as high up as he could (I believe it was to Osborne's) where they were taken by the British—some carried off, according to Simcoe's account, and the rest scattered.

Having been set on shore on the north side of the river, when we arrived in Richmond, I was ordered to take the command of the Magazine and Laboratory at Westham, seven miles above that place.

My brother John joined a fragment of a State regiment, under a Major Ewell, but on the arrival of the Marquis joined a company of his own regiment, under Captain Coleman, and cannonaded Gen. Phillips, then in Manchester, from the heights at Rockets below Richmond.

In a few days after I took the command of the Magazine I saw Mr. Jefferson, then Governor of the State, for the first time; he came to Westham with one of his council, Mr. Blair, whom I had known before, and who informed me they wanted to go into the Magazine. I replied they could not, on which he introduced me to Mr. Jefferson as the Governor. I turned out the guard, he was saluted, and permitted to go in. They were looking for flints for the army of the South, and of the North, and found an abundant supply.

The condition of Virginia can hardly be imagined, her soldiers were nearly all in the army of Gen. Green, her military stores exhausted by constant supplies to the Southern Army—yet there was a spirit and energy in her people to overcome all her difficulties. I was continued in the command of the Magazine. Lord Cornwallis having crossed the James river at Westover, I was ordered to remove it to the south side of the river, and carried it to Brittan's Ferry, on the opposite side of the river, from whence I was ordered to remove it back again to Westham, where it remained until I was ordered to throw the cannon into the creek, and carry the rest of the stores to the Point of Fork, now Columbia—as I did. From thence I was ordered to carry a large portion of the powder and small arms, &c., to Henderson's Ford, now Milton, four miles below Charlottesville; there I remained until Col. Tarleton came to the latter place. There was a Capt.-Lieutenant Bohannan, who had come a few days before, and who ordered me to remain where I was, and defend the Magazine against any detachment that might be sent to take it, until I heard that Tarleton had crossed the river at Charlottesville, after which I should join the Baron Steuben at the Point of Fork. About eleven o'clock, I heard that Tarleton had crossed the river at Charlottesville, and driven away the Legislature. I then commenced my march to join the Baron Steuben.

My orderly, through an interval in the wood, pointed out some of Tarleton's dragoons on the mountain, those that had been sent to catch the Governor Jefferson. I continued my march, but took the Blenheim road instead of the Point of Fork road, by mistake, by which I escaped Tarleton; as he says in his book which I have, that immediately on dispersing the Legislature and Governor, he took the road to the Point of Fork, to meet Lord Cornwallis' Eighth Infantry. By the road I took I was thrown on the South of him, and about a quarter of an hour by sun, I met a man who, on my inquiry, informed me I was five miles from the Baron's encampment, then occupied by Lord Cornwallis' light infantry, who had driven the Baron across the river that morning. Capt. Bohannan having ordered me, if I could not join the Baron, to proceed to Staunton, and from thence to join the corps to which I belonged, in the army of the Marquis La Fayette, I required the man to conduct me to the nearest crossing place on the South branch of James river, by sunrise the next morning, and he conducted me to the mouth of Hardware, and I there crossed the river.

The next day I met Col. Davis, who under the Baron, had the ordering the new recruits and detached parties. I had known him before, and without any salutations, he asked me where I was going. I told him I was going to Buckingham Court-House, to get provisions for the men, for that though I had an impress warrant in my pocket, I did not like to execute it when public stores could be got; to which he replied that Lord Cornwallis' light infantry would be there before me. I said I had left them in the Fork the night before; on which he said "you will do as you please."

Such was the panic every where, that on the next day the soldiers under my command seemed to have caught it, for in turning a lane on our march, some recruits of Capt. Armand's troop came in front, and most of them fled and left me standing in the road almost alone; yet these men had fought under that gallant officer Major Porterfield, at Gates' defeat! They returned, however, to their ranks, and we continued our march to Staunton, to which place I was ordered, as I have said, if I could not join the Baron Steuben at the Point of Fork.

The next day I crossed the Ridge, about six miles to the south of Rockfish Gap, as I now understand, as there is a large limestone spring on the top. When I got to where Waynesborough is, I found a large force of eight hundred or a thousand riflemen, under the command of General McDowell, who Gov. McDowell has told me, was from North Carolina. He stopped me, saying he had orders to stop all troops to defend the Gap. I replied that I belonged to the Continental Army, and had orders to go to Staunton, and said to the men "move on," and he let me pass.

At that time I suppose a regimental coat had never been seen on that side of the mountains—nothing but hunting-shirts—I marched with drums beating and colors flying, and some one seeing the troops, carried the news to Staunton that Tarleton had crossed the mountain, and the Legislature then sitting there ran off again; but learning the mistake, rallied and returned next day.   In the morning I entered the town.   There, for a few days, I heard Patrick Henry, Richard Henry Lee, George Nicholas, and my neighbour Mann Page, of Mansfield. (Though I had heard Patrick Henry before, when I was a school boy in Fredericksburg, in a great case of Mrs. Middleton against a man by the name of Houston, a saddler, for a breach of marriage contract.)   Houston had married a beautiful girl from Caroline county, Miss Johnston, who after the death of Houston married a Major Forsyth, and was the mother of Forsyth, the late Secretary of State.

It may seem strange that so young as I was, not seventeen years old, that I should have the command that I had.   My twin brother, who was an older twin but a younger officer, had left me at Henderson's Ford, being ordered to Albemarle old Court-House, where there were public stores.   I had been in command of about seventy-five men, to guard the Magazine and to make cartridges, post-fire, &c., and when I arrived at Staunton, Col. Davis whom I found there insisted on retaining me in that service, but Capt. Fleming Gaines, who belonged to Harrison's regiment of artillery, ordered me to join my corps as speedily as I could in the army of the Marquis, and furnished me with his horses and servant to do so.

In a few days I left Staunton, and took the road by what is now Port Republic, to cross the Ridge at Swift Run Gap.   A curious incident occurred; one of the horses was taken lame, and I stopped at a smith's shop to have his shoes repaired. The people were all Dutch and spoke no English; seeing me in regimentals, they took me for a British officer, and detained me some time as their prisoner, until one of them came who understood some English, and I showed him my commission, and they let me pass.   At that time Lord Cornwallis having learned that the Pennsylvania line had arrived at Culpeper Court-House, changed his route.   His first design was to burn Hunter's Iron Works, above Falmouth, which were very valuable.   His information must have been very bad; the Pennsylvania line, as it was called, had been disbanded for mutiny in the North, and again recruited, and did not number more than six or seven hundred men, commanded by General Wayne. Gen. Weedon at the same time commanded a small body of militia near Fredericksburg, from which he had nothing to fear in his progress to burn the iron works.   He however, began to retire, when the Marquis re-crossed the Rappahannock at the Raccoon Ford, and by opening an old road threw himself between Lord Cornwallis and our remaining stores in the upper country, and followed Lord Cornwallis at a respectful distance.

The corps of Tarleton and Simcoe in the mean time rejoined him, and he halted but one day on the heights, above Goochland Court-House; where the Marquis also retrograded and placed the army behind Mechunck's Creek—I think they called it, in Fluvanna.   Both armies proceeded slowly towards Richmond, and at Westham I found a corps of which my brother, Robert, afterwards Governor of the State, was a volunteer. He was captured by a troop of Simcoe's regiment, commanded by Capt. Loller.   Lord Cornwallis kept on his way to Williamsburg; and the Marquis halted a few miles below New Kent Court-House, where, on the 4th of July, the army was reviewed and fired a *feu de joie*.

I was attached to Gen Lawson's brigade, with one six pounder, and had some opportunity to know the whole force of the

American army. It consisted of eight thousand militia, Stephen's and Lawson's brigades; of one thousand light infantry, New England troops, brought on by the Marquis, (fine troops they were;) the Pennsylvania line, as it was called, between six and seven hundred men, commanded by Gen. Wayne, with a good train of artillery; one thousand Riflemen, under Gen. Campbell, of King's Mountain, and part of the regiment of Virginia Continental troops, under Colonel Febiger, a Dane; a vidette corps of dragoons, under Captain Larkin Smith; and a single company of Harrison's regiment of artillery, to which I belonged; there were some additional militia, under Major Willis. The British army was more efficient; seven thousand infantry, who had fought the battles of the South; Tarleton's and Simcoe's full regiments of cavalry, and a fine train of artillery. These were all troops that could not be easily driven out of a field of battle. The Marquis, in a few days, marched to the Cross-roads and the Burnt Ordinary, sixteen miles from Williamsburg. (The skirmish at Hot Water, by Col. Butler of the Pennsylvania line, and Major John Willis, with some Virginia militia, had occurred a few days before.)

While the army lay on this ground, Lord Cornwallis marched from Williamsburg to Green Spring, or Jamestown. The morning of that battle, Major George Washington, an old schoolmate, the second aid to the Marquis, was at our quarters, and was asked if the Marquis knew where Lord Cornwallis was, and whether he had crossed the river. His reply was, that Gen. Wayne had been sent on that morning to find out where he was. Tarleton, in his journal says, that one or two days before, he had bribed a white man and a negro to go out, and if they met with any American detachments, to inform them that the British army, except a small portion of it, had crossed the river. It was this negro who fell in with Gen.

Wayne, who on his report, marched down and attacked the whole British army. Tarleton is wrong in supposing that the Marquis intended to bring on a general engagement; on the contrary at 12 o'clock, when he learned that Wayne was in some danger, he ordered Col. Galvan, who belonged to his light infantry, to run down with only one hundred men to his relief, while he, with Capt. John F. Mercer's troop of horse, who had lately joined, and some militia riflemen, followed to support him. The Marquis certainly had no idea of a general battle, as the rest of the army remained quietly in their encampment the whole of the day. General Wayne brought on the battle; relying on the intelligence the negro gave him, whom Tarleton had bribed; for which his troops suffered very much. He, as Tarleton says, attacked the whole British army, and got off only by Lord Cornwallis' supposing that a general action was intended by the Marquis, and taking time to prepare for it. Wayne not only lost his artillery, but had, I think, eleven officers badly wounded, whom I saw the next morning under the hands of the Surgeon, at the church in the rear of our encampment. I think it is very certain that the Marquis, at this time, intended no general battle; nor did Lord Cornwallis either. His object was to cross the river and fall down to Portsmouth, that he might send the reinforcement required of him by Gen. Clinton, who apprehended an attack by Gen. Washington and the Count Rochambeau, who was hourly expected to arrive with the French troops from the West Indies.

(At Williamsburg in 1824, on our return from York, there came an old man by the name of Powell, who had been the Marquis' guide, after the army fell down between the two rivers James and York, and he asked Gen. LaFayette if he remembered the fine horse that was killed under him, at the battle of Green Spring, to which the General replied, the horse was a very fine one, given him by a dear friend of Virginia, who I suppose was Gen. Nelson; but he was not killed under him, he had a leg broken by a six pounder, and he made his bowman cut his throat.)

In a few days after the battle of Green Spring, the single company of artillery of Harrison's regiment to which I belonged, was ordered to the South. It was to proceed to Charlottesville by the way of Goochland Court-House. All the officers except myself, had leave to take their homes in their way, and I was left to conduct the company until they should join at the general rendezvous at Cumberland old Court House, where Col. Febiger, a Dane, an officer in the Continental army of Virginia, an excellent tactician, had the command.

Left to command the company, I felt it a very arduous task, but I had been long enough in service to know that its discipline must be preserved, or I could not command it. The first day's march, we got to the mouth of the lane opposite Hanover Town, and on dismissing the men, I ordered that none of them should go to the town. At retreat beat, in the evening, two Irishmen, Brady and Southerland, on calling the roll, did not answer to their names. I ordered my orderly sergeant to take a file of men, go to town and bring them up, which he accordingly did, and I ordered each of them to receive fifty lashes with the cat-of-nine-tails, at the Gun. That night both of them deserted. Brady I never heard of more, but Southerland was found by my brother John, who had gone home and happened to be in Fredericksburg. He met him in the street, and had him taken and put under guard at the barracks in that town. There had been a draught of militia, and Mr. Page, of Mansfield, had engaged him as a substitute and lost his money, of which he made great complaint. This prompt punishment for disobedience to orders gave me full command of the company, as young as I was.

Having arrived at Goochland Court-House, we were de-

91

tained there, and engaged in making cartridges and port-fire
for some weeks. In the mean time Colonel Davis arrived, and
ordered me to return to Westham, and get the cannon out
which I had been ordered, and had thrown into the creek and
river. He furnished me with a Continental horse, and I found
the officer there had attempted to draw the cannon out of the
mud by fastening ropes to the pieces. I ordered two scows to
be brought, and by pulling the pieces up between them, soon
got them all up and returned to join the company at Goochland Court-House, where I was for some time continued in
command of the laboratory, and finally ordered to Charlottesville, and at last the company reached Cumberland old Court-
House, where it was kept for some time. On my way there my
orderly misbehaved, was put under arrest and tried by a Court
Martial and sentenced to be reduced to the ranks, and to receive one hundred lashes. On the morning of the execution of
sentence, I received a note from Col. Febiger saying he was a
countryman of his, and if I could, consistently with the discipline of the company, dispense with the lashes, he would be
obliged to me. I did so, and in a few days he was again made
the orderly sergeant.

Col. Febiger was an excellent camp officer, well acquainted
with the tactics of the drill, and though I belonged to the artillery, I was called in rotation with other subalterns to train and
drill the infantry, and I acquired perfect knowledge of the
Prussian tactics, written by Baron Steuben, who had been an
aid to the great Frederick. While we were thus engaged, my
brother John and Capt. Fleming Gaines obtained leave to pre-
cede the rest of the troops, and joined the army under Gen.
Green the night before the battle of Eutaw Spring; were in
that battle in the advance, and both acquired some reputation
—indeed, my brother was soon appointed Brigade Major of
the Park of Artillery by Gen. Charles Harrison, who com-

manded it, and lived in the same marquee with him to the end of the war.

The troops at Cumberland old Court-House, were at length ordered to join Gen. Greene, under Col. Posey. Having received no pay, they mutinied, and instead of coming on the parade with their knapsacks, when the general beat, they came with their arms, as to the beat of the troop. A sergeant Hagarltoy was run through the body by Captain Shelton, and Colonel Febiger ordered the barracks to be set on fire, and we marched about eight miles in the evening. I have said the troops received no pay; one company of them, commanded by Alex. Parker, had been taken prisoners in Charleston, had been very lately exchanged, when it received orders to return to the South; the officers received one month's pay in paper, which was so depreciated that I received, as a First Lieutenant of artillery, thirty-three thousand and two-thirds of a thousand dollars, in lieu of thirty-three and two-thirds dollars in specie; with which I bought cloth for a coat at $2,000 a yard, and $1,500 for the buttons. Nothing but the spirit of the age would have induced any one to receive money so depreciated; but we were willing to take any thing our country could give.

We continued our march for about twenty days, having to impress provisions the whole way, in great part of which the country had been foraged by the British, and very little remained to the inhabitants. On approaching Gen. Greene's army, an order came that the infantry under Col. Posey should continue their march and join Gen. Wayne in Georgia. In consequence of this, Col. Posey taking all the wagons, I was ordered to go to the army, lying about twelve miles below, near Bacon's bridge on the Ashley river, to get wagons to take the baggage of the artillery to camp. In that rice country, the great part of which was covered with water, I mistook my way, and swam my horse to the other side of the Ashley river;

meeting with a man on the other side, I asked him how far I was from Gen. Greene's army? to my surprise he told me I was on the wrong side of the river, and that the British had a post at Dorchester. I had to retrace my course, and to swim the river again, where it was very narrow. I proceeded, and obtained the wagons necessary to move the company of artillery, and that joined the Park of artillery. It so happened that I was ordered, with one six pounder, to join the advanced picket, near Bacon's bridge, and it cost me some effort to keep awake the whole night, after so much fatigue. Col. Stewart, of the Maryland Line, was the officer of the day, and came the grand rounds twice in the night, and complimented me on my vigilance.

In a few days my boots were worn out, and I applied to Gen. Harrison for an order on the quarter-master for a new pair; he gave me the order; but said so scarce were the stores that unless Gen. Greene would endorse the order, I would get no boots—and that I must go to headquarters. I accordingly went; he was quartered in a large wooden building, a mile or more in the rear of the army. The first officer I saw when I got there, was his first aid, Major Burnet. He asked if I wished to see the General. I said "yes, I have some business with the General," on which he desired me to sit down, and he would return to me. Having waited some time, I walked to the other door and saw General Greene for the first time, sitting at a table writing. I knew him by his regimentals, and went in. He accosted me, saying, "you belong to the artillery, have you any business with me?" I told him I had an order from Gen. Harrison for a pair of boots, which I wished him to endorse, or I would not get the boots. Looking at my boots, he said, "you have very good boots." On which I replied, I borrowed them that morning: on which he endorsed the order, and I made my bow and left him. He immediately followed me, and overtaking me at the door said, "Lieutenant Brooke, I keep a roster of the officers of the army, and they are invited to dine with me in rotation, and you will be invited in your turn,—but whenever you are off duty, Mrs. Greene will be glad to see you." This arose from the circumstance that Mrs. Greene on her way to join her husband, passed through my neighborhood and received some attentions at Smithfield, and New Post, the seat of Gen. Alexander Spotswood. I was often at headquarters, on this invitation, and felt I was somewhat a pet of the General's. He was a man of most amiable feelings, and showed me marked kindness on one occasion. Capt. Singleton, who was a great favorite of the General's, commanded the company to which I belonged; we lived in the same marquee, on the most amicable terms, until there was a difference between myself and Lieutenant Whitaker, a nephew of his. We were eating watermelons, when I said something that he so flatly contradicted, that I supposed he intended to say I lied; on which I broke a half of a melon on his head, to which he said, "Brooke, you did not think I meant to tell you you lied?" I said, "If you did not, I am sorry I broke the melon on your head," and there it ended. But his uncle, I presume, did not think it ought to have ended there. Whitaker had fought a duel going out with a Capt. Blair, of the Pennsylvania line, and wounded him, which made him, at least in appearance, a little arrogant, and our difference was the talk of the camp.

I had been appointed by Gen. Greene, quartermaster of the Park of Artillery, on the express condition that I should not lose my rank in the line; as I did not come into the army to go into the staff; and having two duties to perform, I was very attentive to that in the line. On one morning when troop beat, I was delayed and did not get on parade till the roll was at least half called, on which Capt. Singleton asked me, in a rude voice, why I was not on parade sooner? to which I replied, "I waited for my boots, and did not come here in gown and slippers," looking at his nephew in that dress. On which he said, he should take another notice of me at another time. The men being discharged, I said to Capt. Singleton, that as long as I thought him my friend, I should have taken a rebuke from him kindly, but as I was now to consider him in a different light, whenever he meant to rebuke me, he must do it through a court martial; that I understood my duty, and was not afraid of a court martial; on which he said he would do so, but never did. After this, we lived together, but never spoke but on duty. I had served with Col. Laurence, who commanded the light infantry in the line, for many weeks; no hint had been given that my staff-office had been neglected; its duties were discharged by the Sergeant Major of the Park, in my absence. No objection had been made by Captain Singleton to the performance of my duty in the line; until the company was ordered to join the light infantry, under Gen. Wayne, to take possession of Charleston on the expected evacuation of it by Gen. Leslie. This was a highly desirable service, and Capt. Singleton seeing me preparing to go, said, "You cannot go, sir, you are quartermaster of the Park." I replied, "I have served in the light infantry before, under Col. Laurence, and no objection was made; but I will go to headquarters and resign that office, rather than not go."

Well, I went to head quarters, and there it was that General Greene befriended me against the influence of my Captain. I stated to him Capt. Singleton's objections to my marching with the company, to join the light infantry, under General Wayne. He said he was sorry that any such difficulty should have been made; "but go into the Adjutant General's office," (who was Col. Harmer, afterwards Gen. Harmer,) "and get a copy of the order appointing you quartermaster of the Park, and show it to Capt. Singleton;" which I did, and that put an end to all difficulty, as the order contained the express condition that I should not lose my rank in the line.

No objection was made to my brother, who was Brigade Major to the Park, and we both marched with the company to join the light infantry under General Wayne. No officer took better care of his troops, and after crossing the Ashley river, he marched us to the Cooper river, to the house, I think, of Col. Wright, who was a refugee; where we were sumptuously entertained, and from his balcony saw the British fleet lying before Charleston.

In the evening, one of the videttes came in and informed General Wayne, that the post called the quarter-house, had been reinforced by four hundred men. This was seven miles from Charleston; a canal was cut there from the Ashley to the Cooper river and two redoubts erected, and the post secured by other fortifications. On the receipt of this information the troops were ordered under arms, and we marched down opposite the quarter-house, within hail of the British sentinels, and encamped in a wood. A flag came out, and as we understood, General Leslie informed General Wayne that he was about to evacuate the town, and, if his rear was pressed, it might be burnt; that if a signal was fired when the troops commenced their march the British troops would be before them, so as to avoid any conflict. Accordingly a six pounder was fired the next morning at daybreak, and we commenced our march for Charleston; the quarter-house was evacuated when we passed it, and in a long open lane we saw the British troops before us. We soon arrived at the Hornwork, where we halted on the draw-bridge, near the gate, which was locked; but Captain Revely leaped over the wall and found the key on the lock, opened the door, and we marched into the town; found all the doors and windows shut, and a British picket still at the state-house, which on the approach of Captain Revely at the head of his company of Maryland light infantry, moved off to the shipping.

General Greene, with Washington's regiment, came in the next day, and the army came down the Ashley river, crossed at Wappoo cut, and encamped on James' Island, opposite Charleston, where the Maryland line, hearing that the preliminary articles of peace had been signed by the British Commissioners, and believing the war over and their enlistment at an end, mutinied. General Greene crossed the Ashley river on hearing it, found them on parade, with their knapsacks, as if the "General" had beat, and ready to march off, as if they were discharged from service. He immediately addressed them, assuring them we had no certain intelligence that the war was over and declaring that he would compel them to return to duty, by the troops that remained firm to their post; and at last prevailed on them to ground their arms, and submit. A few of the ring-leaders were apprehended and, with ropes around their necks, were drummed out of camp.

The artillery to which I belonged remained in Charleston, where we were kindly and hospitably treated, especially myself, by Mr. Frank Kinlaw, who resided at Kinlaw Court; he had been a member of Congress, and married a Miss Walker, of Albemarle county, Va. So kind was he to me, that he invited me to go with him to his estate, near Georgetown, and had provided horses, etc.

When the artillery company, to which I belonged, was ordered under Col. Posey, with the rest of the Virginia troops, to go to Savannah to take possession of it, on its evacuation by Col. Browne, Capt. Singleton, who commanded the company, and my brother, with Lieut. Southall and Lieut. Whitaker, got leave to return to Virginia, and left the company under the command of Capt. Lieut. Booker and myself. On our march to Savannah, Capt. Alexander Parker, who commanded the veteran company of light infantry, and myself, asked leave of Col. Posey to visit a Capt. Day, of the South Carolina line, who resided on the road; which was granted, on condition that we should overtake the troops the next day, which was a march of forty miles, through sandy roads, in the month of April, in that climate.

On arriving in Savannah, the infantry under Col. Posey went four miles below to Thunderbolt, and were quartered there, while the company of artillery was stationed at Fort Wayne, on a point below the town. In Savannah we were most hospitably treated; I mean the officers who remained in town. I felt myself especially noticed; I visited several families, among them Mr. Clay's; he had been a wealthy merchant, and sometime before was a member of Congress. He and his family were particularly kind to me. I gallanted his daughters, one of whom, Nancy, was very handsome. She was about sixteen years of age—but I had no serious intentions. On taking my leave of Savannah, I was left in the room with her by her parents, but said nothing. She afterwards jilted a Mr. Fontaine of Virginia, and married Major Deveau. Fontaine, in despair, went into the army, and in St. Clair's defeat threw himself among the Indians, and was killed.

In Savannah we had balls and dinner parties. There came some English officers from St. Augustine, on flag, with whom I associated; one a Capt. Car, I think. We met in the billiard room, and at Mr. Eustace's, who gave parties. I was at the wedding of Major Habersham with Miss Walton, the daughter of Judge Walton: the entertainment was singular; it was at 11 o'clock in the day, a collation of fruits, wine, and salt fish, &c. I was invited to go into the country with him to a Mr. Gibbs', a few miles from the town, where, having got leave, I spent some very pleasant days.

In Savannah, when invited out, we lived sumptuously;—we had breakfast in the morning, luncheon at 11 o'clock, dinner at two, tea and coffee in the evening, and a hot supper at night. While in Savannah the troops were ordered to an Indian treaty at Augusta, and we were ordered to turn out with whiskers and moustaches; this I was too young to do, being then not nineteen years old; but I used some black pomatum, such as the Hession jägers used, and smeared my face, so as to look very ferocious. The Indians were greatly frightened by their defeat by General Wayne. The night they surprised him, he had given orders that none of them should be captured, that no quarter should be given; yet sixteen of them were captured by Captain Scott's company of the Virginia line; and General Wayne, seeing them next morning, ordered them to be bayonetted; which was deemed by some great cruelty; but General Wayne's force not being so strong as Colonel Browne's, in Savannah, he was obliged to change his position every night, lest he should be surprised by him; and the Indians, who were spies upon his camp, were constantly giving Browne information where he was; but after the defeat and massacre of the sixteen, they quitted the country; they refused to come to any treaty at Augusta, where we were to come, and the corps I belonged to, with the rest of the troops under Col. Posey, were ordered back to Charleston, where we remained till August, when the company to which I belonged, and between three and four hundred of the infantry, and fourteen officers, including myself, belonging to different corps, embarked on board ship for Virginia. We were so long at sea (we were four-and-twenty days out of sight of land) that it was thought in Virginia that we were lost. Having arrived at Hampton, we were most hospitably treated by a Mr. King (who I afterwards knew in the Legislature) and others. After remaining at Hampton three or four days, myself and four other officers were put on board a pilot boat, and came up to Richmond, while the other officers and troops went up in other vessels. When arrived at Richmond, I paid the company off a portion of their pay, which I got of the deputy paymaster, Dunscomb; and then gave them their discharges. I then left Richmond for Smithfield, my home, in a chariot loaned me by Mr. Henry Banks, to take a Mrs. Taylor from Norfolk to Fredericksburg. When we got opposite to Smithfield, I left Mrs. Taylor, took my knapsack, and walked to the house, and found the family at supper. To describe the feelings of joy with which they greeted me, (believing that I had been lost at sea,) would be very difficult.

The Smithfield family at this time consisted of a kind and excellent father; an amiable mother-in-law, who had one son, William, who when he came to man's estate studied law, was successful in his practice, died young, and left an amiable family; my whole brothers, Dr. Laurence Brooke, and Robert Brooke, and my twin brother John.

Dr. Brooke who had studied medicine at Edinburgh, as I have before mentioned, had now commenced the practice of physic. My brother Robert, who had also been educated at Edinburgh, where he had studied law under Professor Miller, had resumed the study, and was preparing to commence the practice of the law when I arrived.

My twin brother John, endeared to me by the hardships and dangers of three campaigns, like myself, had no profession, though some time after he began to study law; got a license, and began the practice of the law; was successful, and became a member of the House of Delegates from his county of Stafford several times. He married a most amiable and excellent lady, and died about the year 1822, leaving a distinguished family,—one of whom, his son Frank, was killed in the Florida war, under Colonel Taylor, now President of the

United States. His son Henry is now a distinguished lawyer
at the bar of the Court of Appeals; and married Virginia, the
daughter of the late Judge Henry St. George Tucker, sometime President of the Court of Appeals.

My only sister married Fontaine Maury, though she had
been courted by Capt. William Washington, afterwards General William Washington, Major Churchill Jones, of Washington's regiment, and several others. Fontaine Maury was the
youngest son of Fontaine Maury, the Huguenot, who came to
this country after the repeal of the Edict of Nantes.

Now what shall I say of myself? The war was over, and
it was time that I should look to some other profession than
that of arms; I was not quite twenty years of age, and like
other young men of the time, having an indulgent father, who
permitted me to keep horses, I wasted two or three years in
fox-hunting, and sometimes in racing; was sometimes at
home for three or four weeks at a time. My father had an
excellent family library, I was fond of reading history, read
Hume's History of England, Robertson's History of Charles
V, some of the British poets, Shakspeare, Dryden, Pope, etc.,
and most of the literature of Queen Anne's reign, and even
Blackstone's Commentaries, before I had determined to study
law. Having resolved at last to pursue some profession, my
brother Dr. Brooke prevailed upon me to study medicine; I
read his books with him for about twelve months, when my
brother Robert would say to me, "Frank, you have missed your
path and had better study law." I soon after took his advice,
and commenced the study of the law with him, and in 1788
I applied for a license to practice law. There were at that
time in Virginia only three persons authorized to grant li-
censes: they were the Attorney General, Mr. Innes, Mr. Ger-
man Baker, and Col. John Taylor, of Caroline; all distinguished lawyers. I was examined by Mr. Baker, at Richmond,

and obtained his signature to my license. I then applied to the Attorney General, Mr. Innes, to examine me; but he was always too much engaged, and I returned home. In a few days after I received a letter from my old army friend, Captain Wm. Barret, of Washington's regiment, informing me that he had seen the Attorney General, who expressed great regret that he had not had it in his power to examine his friend Mr. Brooke; but that he had talked with Mr. Baker, and was fully satisfied of his competency, and if he would send his license down to Richmond he would sign it. I accordingly sent the license to him and he signed it, by which I became a lawyer. I afterwards returned to my brother's office and applied myself more than I had done to the doctrine of pleading, etc.

Early in 1788, I went to Morgantown, in the northwestern corner of the state, then somewhat an Indian country; Virginia being compelled to keep her scouts and rangers to defend the inhabitants on our frontier; though the Indians still made frequent inroads, and killed and carried off five families at the Dunkard Bottom, on Cheat river, twenty miles to the east of Morgantown. I had commenced the practice of the law in the counties of Monongalia, at Morgantown, and Harrison, at Clarksburg. Soon after the district courts were established, and two of the Judges of the district court, Judges Mercer and Parker, came to Morgantown to hold a court there, when I received from the Attorney General, Mr. Innes, a commission as Attorney for the Commonwealth of that District; he having at that time the power to grant commissions to all Commonwealth's Attorneys, in the Districts and Counties of the State.

I continued the practice of the law in that country for a little more than two years, during which time I became acquainted with Albert Gallatin, from whom I not long ago received a letter, written in his eighty-eighth year, which is here inserted:

New York, 4th March, 1847.

My Dear Sir:

Although you were pleased, in your favour of December last, to admire the preservation of my faculties, these are in truth sadly impaired—I cannot work more than four hours a day, and I write with great difficulty. Entirely absorbed in a subject which engrossed all my thoughts and all my feelings, I was compelled to postpone answering the numerous letters I receive, unless they imperiously required immediate attention. I am now making up my arrears.

But though my memory fails me for recent transactions, it is unimpaired in reference to my early days—I have ever preserved a most pleasing recollection of our friendly intercourse almost sixty years ago, and followed you in your long and respectable judiciary career—less stormy, and probably happier than mine. I am, as you presumed, four years older than yourself, born 29th of January, 1761, and now in my eighty-eighth, growing weaker every month, but with only the infirmities of age. For all chronical diseases I have no faith in physicians, consult none, and take no physic whatever.—With my best wishes that your latter days may be as smooth, as healthy and as happy as my own, I remain in great truth,

Your friend,

ALBERT GALLATIN.

Hon'ble Francis Brooke,
Richmond.

I returned to Eastern Virginia, and went to settle at Tappahannock, and practiced law in Essex and the Northern Neck, with Bushrod Washington, afterwards Judge of the Supreme

Court of the United States, Alexander Campbell, a distinguished lawyer, and the old Scotch lawyer Warden, etc.

In that year, the year 1790, I sometimes visited my friends at Smithfield; paid my addresses to Mary Randolph Spotswood, the eldest daughter of General Spotswood and Mrs. Spotswood, the only whole niece of General Washington. Our attachment had been a very early one. Her father frequently sent to Smithfield for me when I was only thirteen years of age; my father would complain, but always permitted me to go. I would find the General, about daylight in the morning, with his fine horses drawn out, and his fox-hounds, and, as I was an excellent horseman, would mount me upon one of his most spirited horses, and often range through the country and woods, where I now live. He knew his daughter was very much attached to me, but though succeeding in my profession, I was but poor, and he had great objections to the match. After some time, however, when I had gone back to Tappahannock, finding his daughter's attachment too strong to be overcome, though she had been courted by others, he consented to our union.

She was sixteen in June, and we were married in October following, at Nottingham, in the year 1791. Her form could not be excelled; her face, when lighted with a smile, was brilliant, though her features were not regular; she had brilliant teeth and luxuriant brown hair; she had been highly educated by a Mrs. Hearn, an English lady, who lived in the family several years. The General was more attentive to the education of his daughters than to that of his sons. He and his brother, John Spotswood, had been much neglected by their guardian at Eton, in England, and were badly educated; they returned to Virginia, and when General Spotswood arrived of age, in 1772, he possessed 150,000 acres of land in the three counties of Orange, Spotsylvania and Culpeper; it was an entailed estate which descended to him from his grandfather, Governor Spotswood. His father's executor prevailed on the Legislature to permit him to sell 70,000 acres of it; he himself afterwards, and before I belonged to his family, sold to Gen. Henry Lee twenty odd thousand acres, above Fredericksburg; he also sold 40,000 acres of leased land to James Somerville, of Fredericksburg. He possessed also iron works; a foundry established by Governor Spotswood, which yielded an income of 5,000 pounds per annum, and which was broken up by his father's executor.

The General was neglectful of his affairs and was better fitted for the army than for the pursuits of civil life. He commanded the second regiment at the battle of Brandywine; and, it was said by a British writer, one Smith, that it was the only regiment that left the field of battle in good order. He was again in the battle of Germantown, where his brother, Captain Spotswood, being badly wounded, was thought to be dead; whereupon he sent in his resignation to General Washington, having made a contract with his brother, when they entered the army, that if either should be killed, the survivor should return home to take care of the two families. When it was known that Captain Spotswood was still alive, a prisoner in Philadelphia, he wished to return to his command in the army; but General Washington replied to his letter to this effect, that he could not be reinstated in his former command, because many officers had been promoted after his resignation. He was soon after appointed a Brigadier General, by the State of Virginia, to command the Legion to be raised in Virginia. During Arnold's invasion, in 1780, he commanded a brigade of militia, called out to oppose General Arnold. General Spotswood spent a great deal of his fortune in the army; and representing a claim for his land, before a committee of the Senate of Virginia, I heard General Meade, who was a member of that committee, say that he knew the fact that while the army of the North was naked of clothing, General Spotswood had clothed his whole regiment out of his own pocket in Philadelphia.

Happily married, with good prospects, we lived together thirteen years, when she died the 5th of January, 1803, after the birth of her youngest daughter, Mary Randolph. She left four children: John, her eldest, Robert, Elizabeth, and Mary Randolph. Elizabeth was unhappily killed by the oversetting of a stage. John studied medicine, and in the year 1825 was appointed a deputy surgeon in the Navy; went out in the *Brandywine*, with General La Fayette, to France, where he had been before; has remained in the navy ever since, and is now fleet-surgeon in the Chinese seas. Robert was educated at West Point, was appointed a Lieutenant of the Engineer Corps; soon resigned, and studied law; began the practice at Charlottesville, went to Staunton, has been twice married, and has a family of eight children. He was twice elected a member of the House of Delegates, from Augusta; was a good speaker, and popular with the House; his family increasing, he declined public life, and is now president of the branch of the Valley Bank, at Staunton.

Mary Randolph was married in 1827 to Dr. Edmund Berkeley, of Hanover; and after many changes of situation, went to Staunton, where she now resides, and has a family of eight children.

The shock I received on the death of my wife I cannot well describe; but my father had left me a legacy better than property, his fine alacrity of spirits (God bless him), which have never forsaken me; and in the summer afterwards I was advised to go to the Virginia Springs, and began to look out for another wife, to supply the place to my children of their mother. While at the Warm Springs, with Mr. Giles and some others, a carriage arrived with ladies; there is something in destiny, for as soon as I took hold of the hand of Mary Champe Carter (though I had seen her before and admired her very much), I felt that she would amply supply the place of my lost wife. I began my attentions to her from that moment. In person and in face she was very beautiful. Mr. Jefferson said of her, "that she was the most beautiful woman he had ever seen, either in France or this country." Her sister Nancy, who married Governor Troup, of Georgia, was thought by some equally handsome. Mary Champe had brilliant teeth and beautiful dark hair; but her beauty was not her only charm; her soft and feminine manners were still more attractive.

On our return to Fredericksburg, I seriously addressed her, and though I had powerful rivals, I soon found that I had won her affections. As I had children, however, her mother and her relations were rather opposed to my pretensions, but their objections were overcome, when they found that our attachment was reciprocal; and we were married on the 14th of February following. Though she had little fortune, her father having left her 1,500 pounds in officer's certificates, (and the half of his plate, on the death of her mother, which by the way she never received,) I had a renewed prospect for happiness. We settled and lived in a small house near her mother's, in Fredericksburg; from there we sent John and Robert to school, to Mr. Wilson, until after the birth of her first son, which she lost. I had built a small brick house with a shed to it, and a brick floor, in the country—her mother and sister went to Boston—when they returned she agreed to come into the country to live in that small house; the farm was a small one and worn out; as I was seldom at home, she had the trouble of planting the hedges, attending to laying off the garden, planting the fruit and house trees, and was frequently at home by herself for five or six weeks at a time. She was always very kind to the parents of her step children, for when Mrs. Spotswood's old cook, Juno, was worn out nearly, they expressed the desire to have our cook, Belissa, who was an excellent one; she readily gave up Belissa to them, and took a girl, little more than seventeen years of age, into the kitchen. She was a kind and affectionate step-mother, and her step-children were very much attached to her. When John had gone to Carlisle College, and then to Philadelphia, and often wrote to me to send him more money, and I being straitened, then she would say, "Send him the money, if you are obliged to sell one of the negroes." When Mary Randolph was sent to her by her grandmother, she expressed as much anxiety for her education as if she had been her own child, and when she grew to a proper age, had a music-master in the house always, and instructed her herself; although she was no performer, she understood music very well.

In 1806, when her health was very delicate and she was advised to go to the Springs, she carried Robert with her, then six years of age; he had had the ague and fever, but recovered at the Springs. We lived forty-two years together very happily, when on the 25th of October, 1846, she expired. She was a sincere Christian, and a quarter of an hour before her death, while I held her feeble hand in mine, she looked up at me and said, "I am not frightened, I am in no pain, take care of ours,"—there she stopped. A short time afterwards when Mrs. Herndon, the wife of Dr. Herndon, who was here attending her, wanted to bathe her lips with cold water, she held out one of her hands and said, "I want nothing more in this world," and expired. She had chosen a burial place; I wrote the epitaph which is engraved upon her tombstone; it is as follows:

(A small but grateful tribute of my heart to one whom I had loved so well and long.)

"SACRED

TO THE MEMORY OF

MARY CHAMPE BROOKE,

THE WIFE OF JUDGE BROOKE;

She expired on the 25th of October, 1846,

IN THE 68TH YEAR OF HER AGE.

She never was excelled in virtue, or any of those endearing qualities which made her an affectionate wife, and devoted mother!"

She left two children, Francis and Helen. Francis married Ella, the youngest daughter of Colonel Ambler. She is a most amiable wife and mother; they have three sons. Helen married most unfortunately, her husband was governed by nothing but passion; treated her very cruelly, and she was forced to apply for a divorce to the Legislature, which she obtained, and now lives with me; and he, like the base Judean, "threw away a pearl richer than all his tribe." She has a little girl, Mary Champe, called after her grandmother.

My native state conferred many offices upon me. I represented the county of Essex in 1794 and '95, in the House of Delegates. In 1796, my brother John having married, and declined the practice of the law, I removed from Tappahannock to Fredericksburg, to finish the law business he and my brother Robert had left. In 1800 I was elected to the Senate of the State, and in 1804, while speaker of the Senate, I was elected a Judge of the General Court, (as my commission will show,) and of course rode the districts of the District Courts, until the Circuit Courts were established; when I was assigned to this circuit, beginning at Goochland, going to Richmond, Hanover, Essex, Caroline and Spotsylvania, until 1811, when I was elected Judge of the Court of Appeals, of which I was President eight years, and where I have continued ever since. In 1831 I was again elected a Judge of the Court of Appeals, under the New Constitution.

My military appointments were as follows: In the year 1796 I was appointed Major of a Battalion of Cavalry, annexed to the second division of the militia. In 1800 I was appointed Lieut. Colonel Commandant of the Second regiment of cavalry, in the second division of the militia, Col. Tom Mann Randolph having resigned. In 1802 I was appointed Brigadier General of the First Brigade and Second Division of the Militia.

Though I had married into two families that had been among the wealthiest in Virginia it did not profit me very much; for though General Spotswood was a devoted father-in-law, he had not much to give me. He gave to his daughter, when we went to Tappahannock, a small servant girl, who soon after died; he gave me a bill of exchange upon Charleston, drawn by Major Churchill Jones, which helped me to purchase an old house in Tappahannock, which was repaired by two of my father's mechanics. In the meantime he wrote a letter to my father, saying that if he would give me ten negroes, of a particular description, he would give me, at his death, an equal share with the rest of his children of his property. My father had delivered some of the negroes before his death, and the General insisted that I should sue his executor for the rest of them; and I brought a suit in the high Court of Chancery, and got a decree for them; in the record of which suit General Spotswood's letter and my father's reply to it can be found. After General Spotswood's death, he having left nothing by his will to me, or any of my family, I brought a suit against his executor, in the Chancery Court at Fredericksburg, upon the contract; but the delays of the law were so great at the time that I compromised the suit with the executor, to which course my counsel, the late Judge Stanard, thinking that I had made a bad compromise, was very much opposed. The executor gave me an order for three thousand dollars on the suit which General Spotswood had in the Federal Court (which suit General Spotswood had against the securities of his guardian,) which ultimately I received. The executor also conveyed to me one hundred and fifty acres of land, which lies near me.

I personally knew, (as well as so young a man could know,) all the eminent military characters of the revolution, with the exception of Alexander Hamilton and General Knox. I knew Washington, Greene and Gates—I knew Washington in my boyhood. He came to Smithfield with General Spotswood, in 1773, I think it was. He was then a Colonel in the British army. I remember his dress; he wore a deep blue coat, a scarlet waistcoat, trimmed with a gold chain, and buckskin small clothes, boots, spurs, and sword; he had with him a beautiful greyhound, was fond of the sports of the field, and proposed to my father, who had a tame deer, to try if the greyhound could not catch him; to which my father assented, and after leaping over the yard palings, they went through the garden where they leaped the palings again; when the deer turned towards the river he got a start of the greyhound, and got into the river before he could catch him. General Washington was afterwards at Smithfield two or three times; he was fond of horses, my father had some excellent ones, so had Gen. Spotswood; they took the horses to the road, and mounted the boys upon them, to try their speed. General Washington, in the year 1774, came to Fredericksburg to review the independent companies. After the review they gave him a collation in the old market-house, where he had all the boys of a large grammar school, of which I was one, brought to him; gave them a drink of punch, patted them upon their heads, and asked them if they could fight for their country. After the war he frequently came to Fredericksburg, where his mother resided, and his only sister, Mrs. Lewis. He attended the ball of the 22nd of February, opened it by dancing a minuet with some lady, then danced cotillions and country dances; was very gallant and always attached himself, by his attentions, to some one or more of the most beautiful and attractive ladies at the balls. The next day, his friends gave him a dinner, at which, after the cloth was removed and the wine came on, a Mr. Jack Stewart (who had been a Clerk of the House of Delegates), a great vocalist, was called upon for a song; and he sung one from the novel of "Roderick Random," which was a very amusing one. General Washington laughed at it very much and encored it. The next day, when I went to his sister's to introduce strangers to him, I found him one of the most dignified men of the age. While he was President of the United States, at the instance of my father-in-law, General Spotswood, he offered me the collector's office at Tappahannock, but I preferred my profession and declined it; though the office at that time was a very lucrative one. Washington was undoubtedly a great man, and there was a sublimity in his greatness which exceeded that of any of the great men of ancient or modern history.

I have said before of General Greene that I was in some degree a pet of his, and I have assigned the cause why I was so. Being a good deal at headquarters, I knew him to be an amiable and excellent domestic character; he was devoted to his wife amid all the danger and excitement of war. And the elder Judge Tucker told me this anecdote of him; that after the battle of Guilford, and the retreat to the Iron Works, the General discovered that he had no bed; he invited him to take a part of his, and in the morning, when Tucker awaked, he found him admiring his wife's picture which hung round his neck. He was much beloved by the army; was cautious not to engage in battle, unless there was a prospect of crippling or defeating the enemy. There is a letter in Johnson's life of him, from General Washington, after the battle of Eutaw Spring, which begins: "I rejoice, my dear General, that you have, at length, gained a victory," etc. I loved him, and to the page of history consign his memory. I did not know Gen. Gates in the Army, but after the peace he resided twelve months in Fredericksburg, and being fond of young company, I frequently saw him; his manners were very fine. He had served in the British army, was, I have no doubt, an excellent camp officer, acquainted with tactics in the drill, but not qualified to command an army.

I have said that I knew also the leading civil characters of that period. I knew Mr. Jefferson very well. The first time I saw him was at the magazine at Westham, above Richmond, as I have mentioned before,—I was afterwards often at Monticello, and saw much of him there; and while he was President of the United States. He was a man of easy and ingratiating manners; he was very partial to me, and I corresponded with him while I was Vice-President of the Society of the Cincinnati; he wished the funds of that society to be appropriated to his central college, near Charlottesville, and on one occasion I obtained an order from a meeting of the society to that effect; but in my absence the order was rescinded, and the funds appropriated to the Washington College, at Lexington, to which General Washington had given his shares in the James River Company, which the State had presented him with. Mr. Jefferson never would discuss any proposition if you differed with him, for he said he thought discussion rather rivetted opinions than changed them. When I was elected Speaker of the Senate of Virginia he sent me his parliamentary Manual, with a very flattering note wafered in it, which is now in the possession of my son Robert. Of Mr. Madison I personally did not know as much; his manners were not so fine or insinuating as Mr. Jefferson's; he was devoted to Mr. Jefferson, but differed with him in some respects; he never shunned discussion, but courted it—told many excellent anecdotes of times past—and was among the purest and ablest statesmen we ever had. I knew Mr. Monroe; practiced law with him, and I think, though a slow man, he possessed a strong mind and excellent judgment. When I was at York, in 1824, with General La Fayette, Mr. Calhoun, then Secretary of War, was there, and I asked him the question whether it was the President Monroe, or his Cabinet, who were in favor of that passage in his message which declared to the Holy Alliance that America would not be indifferent to any attempt to aid the Spanish Government to prevent the enfranchisement of the South American Provinces, then at war with Spain; and he replied that it was the President's own sentiment, and that though he was a slow man, yet give him time and he was a man of the best judgment he had ever known.

This Narrative has been written, or dictated, by snatches, at different times, and may therefore contain some repetitions, and I may have omitted some things that ought to be in it; but my recollections are too numerous for me to record them all, and I believe I have given a sufficient number of them to answer my purpose—to gratify my family and friends—and I will now rest.